The Twelve-Dollar GRILL

The Twelve-Dollar Dollar GRILL

A lifestyle philosophy change
that will make you more fulfilled.

JACK RACKAM

To order additional copies of this book, contact:
Xlibris Corporation
1-888-795-4274
www.Xlibris.com
Orders@Xlibris.com
48658

Contents

To my family and loved ones, both alive and those who have passed on. I am sorry for the past fifty-one years of letting you down. Maybe I have enough time left to make it all right.

PREFACE

I clearly learn everything the hard way. I call it the hands-on failure method. When I was in college and really needed to study and truly learn something, I would write everything down and work through the concepts with drawings, examples, or whatever type of writing was needed to address the topic. The act of putting concepts into written form somehow helped solidify them into my memory. Writing also helped me understand the reasons behind the answers rather than simply memorizing them.

As you will see herein, I obviously had a difficult time learning many life lessons. I wrote this book to force myself to put on paper my failures and the lessons that I have learned from these failures. I have high hopes that the learning process from my college days will once again work and commit to my permanent memory the many life lessons that have eluded me for fifty-one years.

If by writing down my failures and the lessons that I have learned I also help one other person learn a little about life, then I will have done a really good thing. For that reason, I published this homework project. Every word herein is a true recount of events in my life and is completely nonfiction. That this is true is a bit embarrassing to me, but it is the fact of the matter. My hope and prayer is that no one will have to go thru what I have put myself and my family through, and if what I share with you here is able to help others, I will have accomplished my goal.

CHAPTER 1

LIFE IN THESE UNITED STATES

Any reasonable, fair-minded review of our lives in the United States today would have to question the real quality and quantity of our lives and lifestyles. Without question, we have material things, technology beyond belief, and advertised excitement around every corner. Yet I do not meet many people who proclaim to be happy. They are stressed, unhappy with their jobs, their children are problematic, or their family life is suffering from either financial stress or one of the partners is being—or is about to be—unfaithful. No one today seems content or happy or seems to be enjoying a world that offers everything that can be imagined. Clearly, our children are not projecting a happy existence as evidenced by the alarming rate of school violence, suicide rates, depression rates, and other statistics that dominate our daily newscasts.

It is this state of affairs that made me look at my life from afar to determine whether I appeared to everyone else as they appeared to me. Overall, I concluded that I too was relatively empty, bored, unhappy, and dissatisfied with my life. To understand why, I looked around at my little world and concluded the following. These conclusions are not scientific or results of controlled surveys or Gallup Polls. These are my simpleminded, commonsense conclusions gleaned from an average, small-town person's perspective using the most accurate means of evaluation, common sense, and observation.

FAMILY VALUES

I was raised in a small town in the '50s and '60s. Back then, children had manners or else. They had to do daily chores, had to respect their elders and parents, had to be forced to behave at school, had to dress respectfully, and generally had to reflect and act like a young man or woman. There were consequences if these ideals were not followed. The parents and the school system worked in tandem to mutually enforce and instill these values into children. There were, of course, children who did not measure up as is always the case. For the most part, the majority fell into the mold and learned—intentionally or accidentally—basic manners, respect, and the reasonable boundaries of living and working with others.

Because this era was my era, it is my comfort zone and my benchmark for children today. More importantly, it was the type of child raising that spawned the generation of people who created the most dramatic changes in American history. Technology, productivity, and all sectors of our world have advanced logarithmically under the watch of the children raised the way I was raised. So I have to conclude that it was successful and worth doing and a reasonable methodology. In simple words, it worked.

That era of success then bred a new generation of both parents and children. No longer do we have dinner together or spend Sunday afternoons visiting with family and friends or at wholesome social functions. We do not have porch visits with our neighbors, and in many cases, we do not even know our neighbors. Manners, respect, decent dress codes, and a general feeling of goodwill do not appear to readily exist now. Our children act as if a good life is an entitlement rather than a personal goal for which they have to work. Children are not learning until it is too late that there are consequences to everything, good and bad. Children speak to their parents in tones and volumes that in my era were tantamount to a "kiddie life sentence." I cannot imagine the repercussions that would have resulted to me in my childhood if I had treated my parents or teachers with the disrespect that seems to be the norm today. How did this attitude gain such a foothold in our society? We have created a "tail wags the dog" environment in which everyone but the average middle-class American has to be protected from possible offensive titles regardless of their accuracy.

Marriage is at an all-time failure rate, probably because finding those greener pastures is much easier now than in the past. Functioning on the theory that it is easier to quit than to work through a problem is also more the norm than the exception today. Divorce is now a simple, routine process without any negative social consequences. Since sports heroes and Hollywood figures do it all the time, it must be acceptable—and even possibly the "in" thing to do. That is the prevailing perspective, or cop-out, regardless of which side you are on. Because of the numerous divorces, one-parent and stepparent households are crumbling at the edges, resulting in a basic breakdown in the child-raising process. According to the U.S. National Center for Health Statistics' annual *Vital Statistics of the United States* and *National Vital Statistics Reports* (vol. 54, no. 20, July 21, 2006) and prior reports, in 2005, for every one thousand of population, there were 7.5 marriages and 3.6 divorces.

Schools and teachers have lobbied and have obtained zero-tolerance rules that apply to all situations regardless of the similarity of the facts of each situation. (There is a need for rules such as these for clearly and completely unacceptable conduct, such as carrying a gun to school, but these are not the rules I am referring to here.) These rules give teachers an easy way out when addressing situations meriting punishment as they allow harsh punishment to apply across the board to all persons without regard to the individual circumstance of each incident. I once knew a student who was struck in the head from behind in the lunch line, and he fell to the floor. As was his natural instinct, he stood up and took a swing at the attacker but did not strike him. However, because the rule stated that all students in fights must be expelled, both students were dismissed from school. There is something patently wrong with dealing with children in this manner. Clearly, both needed some form of punishment, but how could such rash punishment apply equally to each student? Refusal to look at each child in the situation on his or her own merits teaches children that the use of judgment and common sense is no longer needed. Analysis has become a lost art. As more and more punishment that does not fit the crime is doled out, respect for rules in general and for those enforcing them diminishes, which cannot have positive consequences. We were given brains and the tools of judgment and common sense. A litany of bright-line rules can never adequately replace such wonderful tools.

As noted earlier, many households today are one-parent homes or stepparent homes in which all parents work. In these homes, rules are made in good faith, but enforcement breaks down because parents have limited time with their children. In most such homes, the time that the family has available for quality interaction has been reduced drastically. Babysitters or day care centers often raise our children, and parents do not want to spend what little time they have at home with their children disciplining them; they do not want to play the role of "enforcer." As a result, parents make rules but do not consistently follow through with them, sending a myriad of wrong messages to young children.

Add this type of home environment to the change in the philosophy of our school system wherein they are not the partner that they were in my era to share discipline and character-building responsibilities, and one can easily see how our society has left many of our children without the support system needed to learn the right values that became second nature to my generation. From my perspective, our system is not working. Moreover, what time parents do have available for their children is often spent watching them play or practice sports. I ask, "What value does that have toward raising your children the right way?" Instead, if time is an issue, let the kids play while you get your work done; and then spend one-on-one time with them when they get home. Do not allow the judgment of society dictate that you are a bad parent if you are not at every game and every practice session. Ideally, a parent can attend all events; but sometimes, life is not that generous with time and money, and parents need to make smart choices.

According to an article written by Myron Magnet and published by CNNMoney.com, on August 10, 1992, the following statistics help explain possible causes of the attitudinal issues of and problems with our children today. The article points out that during the '50s, the divorce rate fell to 11 percent, or 9.2 per thousand married women. In the '60s and '70s, the rate skyrocketed to 22.7 per thousand married women. At that time, 57 percent of divorced women had children under the age of eighteen. The article also cited evidence that, later in their lives, these children had trouble forming intimate, loving relationships. The article echoed the fact that the economic pressures of the times had begun forcing both parents in households to work and that this clearly had a negative effect on the family unit and parenthood in general. In its entirety, the article addresses in depth most of the issues I raise herein. And although actual statistics are interesting, we are well aware that these issues are real. The question is, "What do we do about it?"

We need to overlay these issues with the advancements in today's world and their effects on this generation. As noted earlier, there is a rising attitude of self-absorption and self-thought. Given the proliferation of cell phones, MySpace, computer games, and the availability of the Internet in general, we are isolating our children and allowing them to interact with others without in-person contact. Children do not even talk on their cell phones; instead, they "text" one another. They have even created an entirely new language of abbreviated words and phrases to further limit the personal interaction. They communicate and share ideas through a Web site called MySpace rather than getting together in person and just doing a show-and-tell. They spend their days indoors playing computer games, talking with or texting one another on their cell phones or on MySpace rather than being outside playing, getting exercise, being with other children, and learning how to act with and react to others. My fear is that these impersonal modes of communication will interrupt and block the development of interpersonal skills used in personal interactions. I fear that these new means of communication will damage our children's ability to communicate with others and to understand others.

Spending time interacting with others remains the only real way to get to know them. In fact, one can very easily hide or disguise who one really is if the most communication and interaction that one has with others is on the phone or through the computer or another such device. There is a funny video out on this issue. In the video, the guy posts a very cool and sexy profile of himself on his Web site and communicates with others using this persona. In reality, he is the stereotypical nerd. Without personal interaction, there was no way to know that he was not as his computer personality showed him to be. Personal interaction is the only way to learn how to get along and grow. Yes, the Internet has given us great learning power and has opened doors of knowledge that were never dreamed of just a few years ago, but that does not address the big picture. Allowing your child to spend immense amounts of time on the computer is like facing the old dilemma of whether your child should go away to college or stay home and go to a local two-year college. Many factors go into this decision, such as finances and maturity of the child; but most people will agree that the on-campus experience of living and dealing with the everyday issues of others, finances, scheduling, priorities, self-discipline, and other real-life situations are some of the greatest lessons a child can learn—especially when the family is close by to help out when things go too wrong or are about to. So in this new age or era, we need to again address this entire topic in a different disguise. I doubt that anyone can claim that they know the ultimate outcome or the best way to deal with it, but it is here to stay.

Clearly, parents do not behave in any of the above ways intentionally or maliciously. Our current society has burdened us with these issues. Granted, life in the '50s and '60s was no way nearly as complicated. Thus, the issues we face now were not issues facing parents of that time. And this is what I am pointing out. How and why we got here is an important discussion, and being mindful of that may help in finding ways to better deal with the day-to-day parenting issues of today's society. I also believe that many of the parenting and family-related issues that we face today form the basis of the unhappiness and dissatisfaction with life that I observe in many people today.

GOVERNMENT

Would anyone not agree that, in modern times, the representative form of government has lost its representative nature? We elect our government by popular vote, but the media and political action money control who runs and what the agendas are once in office. No person can be elected and actually do what he or she feels is best for the people they serve, let alone do what their voters want done.

This whole situation is worsened by the general attitude that "my vote means nothing, so why make the effort to vote?" Not many people care enough to write a letter, make phone calls, or start a grassroots effort to change things that are wrong. The people would continue to rule this world once they get themselves back into the game. Until then, special interest is the king.

On top of all of this, if a good candidate can work his way through the financial gambit and raise the money to run and neutralize the committees and get them off his back, then the media would find something to sell papers and airtime with and ruin him before his agenda gains full steam. This is just the way of the current world and must change. The circle of politics in Washington has to stop, and a new course must be charted. This cannot be done quickly or easily. However, over time, this change must begin; and if we are diligent and persistent, it will work.

Regardless of who is in power, our government spending is beyond reasonable understanding. First, government accounting is not based on income or productivity or results. It is based on budgets. As an accounting student in college, government accounting was the only course that I found difficult. That there are no standards once the budget is set to control the money available baffled me. Such an approach results in wasteful and unnecessary year-end spending. To understand this, just ask anyone you know in a government position what happens at year-end when there is excess money in their budget. It gets spent on something. The belief is that if it is not spent, their budget will be reduced the following year. A system must be implemented to protect one's budget if frugal measures are employed. I do not have the answer, but someone out there can figure this out, and it needs to be done. We must employ reasonable financial management if we are to survive and remain a world power.

Couple this ridiculous concept with our tax situation as the two are clearly related to each other, and we see the real problem facing our children and grandchildren. Currently, the average person has to work until some date in April just to pay that year's taxes. Proper management of our country's money would help drastically in this regard.

Let's take immigration. Is this not the biggest boondoggle you have ever seen? Is there any way out of the mess? I will not belabor the issue, and I clearly do not have the answers, but how did it get this bad before someone addressed it? We pay dearly to fund the border patrol and the other agencies that monitor this situation, yet we now have a full-scale mess without solutions right under their noses. While this problem continues, the IRS is hounding legitimate citizens and legal businesspeople and allowing illegal workers and their employers to get away with paying no taxes at all. Something is wrong with this picture. Our priorities are out of order, and this needs to change.

Again, I ask the question, "Could some of these issues be the cause of what I see as a generally unhappy populate?"

FINANCES

What family do you know that does not fit into one of the following categories?

1. They have a variable rate loan that started at 4 percent or 5 percent but can increase to 14 percent.
2. They have credit card debt over $15,000.
3. At least one spouse works two jobs.
4. They have a second mortgage HELOC loan on their home, burdening their home with debt close to, if not exceeding, current market value.
5. They are faced with more than one of these situations.

Our affluent society has created a "keep up with the Joneses" mentality. We must have everything the other person has, go to the same vacation spots, and frequent the same restaurants and clubs. That we have to beg, borrow, and steal to keep up this lifestyle seems not to matter. Desiring and dreaming of nicer things and better homes and picturesque vacation spots is natural, but to actually buy them when doing so puts a burden on a family structure already about to blow at the seams is problematic.

We are borrowing ourselves into debt to buy a gas-guzzling SUV, to take an exotic vacation, to keep our kids in the coolest clothes, and to give them iPods and cell phones. Doing these things does not add happiness, just stress. Moreover, this kind of spending teaches our children wrong financial habits and gives them the false impression that the so-called good life is the norm, not a goal to strive and work for. Additionally, we now have to work harder and longer to stay financially even, leaving us with no time to enjoy our families or the things we just purchased.

Think about it. Of all of your friends, or yourself, who bought a $50,000 four-wheel drive SUV, how many times have you gone off road and used the vehicle for its intended purpose? Have you ever even engaged the four-wheel drive? Have you ever used the winch on the front bumper or those blinding lights on the roof for any real purpose other than to show other people that you have them? Why did you buy the vehicle? It was clearly not for its function. You bought it to impress others with your status symbol. Why? Whom are we trying to impress? As for those exotic vacations, how many times have you reviewed the photos after you looked at them the first time? Other than to brag to your friends, do you have time to stroll down memory lane and see your children's faces in those photos later in life? No, because we do not have time to enjoy the memories we create. Did you really have a good time on the vacation since you had to be careful with spending because your credit card was full from purchasing the trip? Was it a family outing, or did the parents go their way and the children went theirs? Was it really fun, or was it a marathon to try to jam everything into a few days and spend time buying T-shirts so that everyone back home knew you went to this place?

All in all, is it not true that as your income rises, your standard of living follows? Of course, this is true in most families. As a result, one is left with no greater savings account, no less debt, and just a heavier burden to carry. I couch the question like this, "Do my steaks and hamburgers taste any better on a $3,000 stainless steel gas grill than they do on a $12 charcoal grill?"

It comes down to this. Do the things we buy and the places we go make us happier or sadder, more relaxed or more stressed, better people or worse; and do they enhance our family life or add more stress to it? Depending on the answers to these questions, we need to evaluate what we are doing with the little money and time that we have.

To continue our theme, let me point out that issues like these also contribute to the general unhappiness in our culture that I have observed.

The foregoing are my personal observations and conclusions from a specific look at my life and at the lives of the many friends and associates with whom I am acquainted. They clearly do not apply to everyone, nor does everyone and every family fall into the generalizations that I set forth. Government is not in ruins; it just needs some serious attention. There are many dedicated, loyal, and moral people in many areas of our political structure. The world is not in financial ruin, but it needs to be looked at, and some adjustments need to be made. I do not have a doom-and-gloom outlook, and I am not a cynic. I simply want to raise a few well-founded questions that seem relevant in my inquiry into where we are today and how we got here.

So how did we get here, and where are we going? Since our country is a country of average people, let's take a trip from the '50s and '60s to the millennium through the life of an average American—me. This journey may help explain and put into perspective our current situation and state of being.

If we can gain an understanding of where we are and how and why we got here, I cannot help but think that we can find a better course that will lead us to happier and more fulfilling lives. My introspection has helped me improve and add meaning to my life, and I hope that it does the same for you.

CHAPTER 2

EARLY CHOICES

I was born into a relatively normal lower-middle-class family with my dad as the only employed parent outside the home. My parents divorced when I was seven, and we moved in with my grandparents who became my pseudoparents while my mother began a career. My mother remarried when I was thirteen and moved to Atlanta, giving me the choice of living with her and my new stepfather or my grandparents. I chose the known quantity and environment and did not move to Atlanta with her.

My respect for my grandfather, then age seventy-two, was enormous. Failing or disappointing him was my greatest fear. That respect replaced the fear of punishment that I would have had in a normal home environment. My grandfather was in great health and was as active as any fifty-year-old father. We played ball and went hunting, fishing, and swimming. In most respects, he was as much of a father figure as my natural father was.

My grandfather raised me to follow three basic principles: (1) most anything in moderation is acceptable, and nothing in excess can be good; (2) follow the Golden Rule; and (3) for actions, there are equal and opposite reactions called consequences.

To have other than the basic needs and requirements, I had to work. I mowed grass, cut tobacco, and did miscellaneous seasonal jobs. I was expected to get good grades, and my behavior was to be well above average. I followed these guidelines quite well, with only a few notable failures; and when those happened, rule number 3 was applied.

As a child, I was raised to go to church, Sunday school, and Bible school. I said my nightly prayers and the "blessing" before meals. It was routine and scripted. The sermons almost every Sunday were about "fire and brimstones" and money. Hardly a Sunday went by when those topics did not dominate, and the collection plate was stressed for either a building project or foreign aid missions. The preacher was always giving you the meaning of the Bible and telling you what Jesus, God, and the other biblical characters were saying and meaning.

Even as a child, it occurred to me that there were an awful lot of man-made rules and interpretations to religion. I could not understand why my friends who were Baptists, Presbyterians, members of the Church of God, Lutherans, or those of other religions believed differently; yet they used the same Bible, and all claimed that their way was the way to God and heaven. It seemed that not all roads could lead to heaven, but I just assumed I would understand the inconsistency when I got older. Why could Methodists dance and Baptists not? Why could Catholics drink and others not? When I raised these issues, I got the answer, "You just have to have faith!" But in what? Which version of the Bible? Which denomination? Who was more correct? If Jesus was Jewish, was that not the best choice? All of this confused me, and no one had the answers to such questions from a young child. I believe that this dilemma kept me from really digesting and implementing the teachings of the Bible and understanding God. The religious establishment had not figured out how to address these issues, and as a result, many of their lessons fell upon my deaf ears. I now understand that this failure ultimately contributed to the catastrophic failures of my life, but more on that later.

It was from this environment that I graduated high school and went directly to college that summer. I applied my grandfather's principles and, while working through school, graduated with a four-year accounting degree in three and a half years then entered law school and graduated with a three-year degree in two and a half years. In each case, I maintained a 3.5 GPA or higher.

My choice to major in accounting and then a legal career was based primarily on my family's intervention. They knew that I was naturally good with numbers and logical thinking, and they guided me as best they knew into these fields.

Let's think about life today. As the family interaction and interrelationships have changed, so has the method used by young people in making their choices. Personally, I do not believe that parents today know their children as well as my mother and grandparents knew me. Moreover, the choices made today seem to be driven more by the child's perceived desires and his or her opinion of where he or she should go than the opinions of the parents. Recently, a counselor at the local high school told the eighth-grade class that they needed to decide on their careers so that they could take the right classes, which would thereby help them get into the proper college. I ask, "How do we expect thirteen-year-old children to know what their career paths will be?" Advising them to select a career so early in life puts untold pressure on such young minds. However, this is the environment that our children grow up in. The competition and pressure to succeed and get ahead starts way too soon in their young lives.

So today, we have young people eighteen to twenty-two years of age, or much younger who, by definition, lack the experience and judgment to make decisions like this. And they are being allowed to make such life-altering choices as follows:

1. The choice of college or no college
2. The choice of a major if college is chosen
3. The choice of employment if no college is pursued
4. The choice of marriage and when
5. The choice of children and when
6. The choice of debt or no debt early in life
7. The choice of living in an apartment or purchasing a home

It is possible, and is generally the rule, that by a person's early twenties, he or she is heavily in debt in relation to their income, is married with children, and is in a career that he or she chose at the ripe old age of between eighteen and twenty-two. This is a very serious situation. Many times, things work out; yet many times, they do not. I think it is safe to say that more people than not would admit that their chosen career, or lack thereof, is not really what they expected or anticipated. Further, many will admit that they long to take a different course but cannot given the current situation that their early choices leave them in. Clearly, from looking at the divorce rates, statistics support the theory that marriage was clearly not in line with their expectations.

Every day, we place children into the ship of life without also giving them the safety equipment and navigational skills that they need to make a successful journey. I'm not saying that this has never been how parents have moved their children from childhood to manhood. However, I have observed that changes in the family structure have limited the ability of parents to prepare their children for lifelong choices. I also believe that societal pressures force certain decisions on children that are not in their best interests.

Heavy debt early in a marriage is a recipe for disaster. Add children to that, and the result is 200 percent more stress and anxiety on the family. Children are a true blessing; however, other choices in life can cause the birth of children to create many problems that can be avoided with forethought and common sense.

Again, I am simply pointing out that without a solid family and school life, young people are being put into a very hostile environment at a very vulnerable time in their lives. We need to strive to help them with their early life choices as much as we can. Once they sign that marriage certificate, car-loan agreement, home mortgage, and birth certificate, their course in life is virtually set—and that is scary. If I am correct in stating that, in general, our current populate leans toward the easy way as opposed to the harder, more prudent course, then maintaining the status quo is what people do rather than realizing their mistakes and take the time and effort to improve their situations to be more in line with their true desires. If this is the choice people are making, there is no way to truly be happy.

I was sent off into the world with a good set of navigational tools and skills and on a safe vessel. Many today are not. Yet as you will see later, even what I had is not always enough, but it is a good start.

Relating back to the first chapter, I conclude that, in many cases, we as a current society are victims of this very problem. To fix it, we need to begin at the ground level. We need to instill real values and goals in our children. This needs to be done both in the home and in the schools. We must make sure the family is real, and that it is an important factor in every child's life. We must be consistent, and doing this will give the children their best shot at a truly good life, one filled with success and happiness.

CHAPTER 3

LATER REALITIES

Although the initial choices I made in my life were good ones during the years after college, I fell victim to the times. By the early '80s, everything was great. Money was behind every door, and opportunity was everywhere. I was hardworking and eager, went after the gusto of life, and forgot the three principles that had been ingrained in my soul since childhood. I married my high school sweetheart; and even though she was a wonderful person, we were just best friends, not husband and wife. I acquired debt to get into venture after venture in pursuit of the "good life." As a result, by age twenty-six, I was in debt up to my proverbial eyeballs, divorced, and miserable. I had pushed way too hard. I fell victim to following the easy and fun path and failed to demonstrate character and conviction for right and proper values and principles. I overlooked the feelings of others and never stepped back to do any self-evaluation. I saw my successes as being a result of my efforts and my failures as being generally the fault of others.

I was happy with my career as a small-town attorney, but everything else in my life was awful. My fight for the "good life" had cost me the result of a truly good life—happiness. I see many people today living like this. My excellent childhood had been overcome by the current day's desire for material things and fulfilling unhealthy wants. If the influences of today could corrupt my childhood teachings, no wonder it can adversely affect our children.

As I looked at my situation, all I could do was push forward and try to start again. At least I had a career to lean on. What I did not realize was that my push to get good grades, get out of school quickly, and get into the working world left me wanting to be a kid again, to do reckless things, and to behave irresponsibly. I had skipped through my normal childhood, and that was now showing. I had made a choice—I had grown up too fast, which seemed an excellent choice at the time but was coming back to haunt me. I forgot principle number 1—most anything in moderation is acceptable, and nothing in excess can be good. I had gone past moderation in my life and was about to violate principles 2 and 3.

CHAPTER 4

PREPARED TO GO NOWHERE

Until now I had, with the help of my family, prepared myself. I had received an excellent education, had developed excellent communication skills, and had above-average people skills. I had made some bad choices right out of school, but I knew that I was young and could overcome them. However, my choice to move back home and to a small-town law practice caused me to believe that I was going nowhere. I had had many offers of other employment and all of them in larger cities, but I had found reasons to turn each of them down. Yet regardless of my current doubts, it was a solid career with decent money, but the issues and legal questions that arose were common and unchallenging. There was no real room to earn a large salary, and there was no upward mobility. I felt like I was living the pinnacle of my career with nothing more to look forward to. Therefore, I had to create challenges.

I saw the world as a constant challenge, a series of goals linked together. For me, once I accomplished one goal, I started on the next. Downtime, family time, church time, public service time, and just helping a friend work on his fence were not important to me. These things could wait, and I had plenty of time for them after I had made my first million. As a result, my constant pushing prevented me from seeing the wonderful life that I actually had.

I believed that I had made the easy, safe choice in my youth to go home to a small-town family practice. I had "settled" and had not challenged myself. I had underachieved. This was how I saw myself at that point in my life. I was upset with myself and felt like I had turned a good choice into a mediocre one. I became bored, dissatisfied, and restless. I began doing side deals to make more money and to challenge myself. I formed a construction company and built many homes, invested in high-risk deals for the excitement, and bought and sold real estate. These activities brought out the extreme in me and gave me the income level I believed that I needed.

Along with this mentality came the girls, the clubs, drinking, and generally living like a college kid again. Once again, I had violated principle number 1. That extra income slipped away because my excesses put me back into the same relative position of income to debt. I just had to work harder to stay in the same place. I had more stress, less sleep, and more problems in my life.

On one of my big nights out and after I had consumed a lot of alcohol, I was a passenger in a very horrible auto accident. My face had been crushed, I had a tear in my dura that caused a major leak of spinal fluid, I had broken my leg, and I was about to die. I was in intensive care for eighteen days, in the hospital for a total of four weeks, and had four postrelease surgeries to get me back to almost normal. I missed six months of work—and the income that went along with it. Most of all, I almost lost my life.

While in the hospital, I got to know my "married" nurse, with whom I became involved. She divorced, and six months later, she and her seven-year-old daughter helped me set up a home for the second time. I settled down in my stepdad/husband role and started life again. My financial situation had not improved; in fact, with her spending habits, it worsened. That, coupled with a new family, added more stress and burden to my life. We got along great for a while, but she was clearly feeling the same stress. Instead of talking about it, she took up drinking—and a lot of it. Add in a few drugs along the way, and wife number 2 was out of control. We engaged counselors and others to try to help her, but our marriage was soon beyond repair, and I was divorced again. I felt, however, that I had given this second marriage a real shot. I had taken great care of the child and in fact took the child into my custody for eight months after the divorce while the mother entered rehab. I had not failed that duty, and fatherhood was a wonderful experience for me. Later in life, after my stepdaughter graduated college, she found me and told me how much she appreciated that I was in her life. Although I did not get that pat on the back for fifteen years, when it came, it retroactively made marriage number 2 worthwhile.

At the time of my second divorce, it was clear to me that I had wasted nearly one-third of my life. In reality, I was much worse off then than the day I had graduated high school. I had blown my gifts and opportunities. I had wasted the precious love and trust that my family had given me. I had lost my engine and anchor; and as most sailors know, when that happens, you will find rocks ninety-nine times before you accidentally drift into paradise. I was on the rocks, and the winds were howling, and I was going nowhere.

I had forgotten the three principles that I had been raised with. I continued to work hard, but for the wrong reasons. I tried to do too much and be too many things to too many people. I indulged in excesses. All that was left to do was to pick myself up and glue the pieces back together. I just had to.

The good news is that I had subconsciously learned some valuable lessons that would surface later in my life. I learned to love and care for another person. My stepdaughter was a helpless and vulnerable child. Although a brief encounter, she and I had created a bond, and we connected. From this, I learned the value and benefit of family and of helping others. I learned that selfless love could be a wonderful thing. I learned that I was not the most important thing in the world. Of course, these lessons had to sink in; and until something brought them to the surface, they remained hidden in my strong-willed personality. But I did learn them, and they were cataloged in me. As you will see later, they flourish when I most needed them.

CHAPTER 5

SUSPENDED ANIMATION

I buckled down and really threw myself into my work. I knew that I needed to find the right partner and get back on track. About two years later, she walked into my office to interview for a job. We both knew that it was the right fit from the start, and after a while, we were married. Wife number 3 and I worked hard together, had soon solved all of our financial issues, and began to properly enjoy life together and with our families. We went to church, visited family on Sundays, and traveled with her parents and sister. I was building a good practice and had gained the respect of most of my peers and the people of my little town. I had finally made it back. It had taken the help of many people, I had dedicated myself to the original principles of my life, and it had all come together.

But with all good things come the bad; and the Gemini, as I am, deals with its two personalities. My life was good, but it was like the movie *Groundhog Day*. Every day brought the same routine, and there were no challenges. Same breakfast, same schedule, same people, same everything.

Right on cue, a client with a large international business and a patented, government-mandated one-of-a-kind product found themselves on the verge of bankruptcy. With their products and patents, I believed that we could find a buyer for the business. After visiting many potential buyers all over the country, we discovered that no one wanted to invest money because of the client's dire financial conditions. No one, not even the large investment firms, could think outside of their Excel spreadsheets and the ratios they spit out—a lot like the zero-tolerance rules discussed earlier. Judgment and common sense had been taken out of the business world. Nonetheless, the hammer of the bank was on its way down.

On New Year's Day, the family called and asked that since I had the idea if I would invest and take the company over to get it sold. Such an investment was to have taken every dime that I had and a large note to boot. But I decided that this was my chance and dove in. In nine months, after many sleepless nights and working 24/7 on the problem, we sold the largest division of the company for millions. We had done it. What all of the big boys said was impossible had become a reality. The many large brokerage companies who had laughed openly to our faces had been wrong. And for me, this was my last-second touchdown in my Super Bowl. I made a large sum of money. In fact, I made more money in those nine months than in the prior forty-five years of my life. I had made it. My state of suspended animation was over.

CHAPTER 6

UPKEEP, TOYS, AND THE GRINDSTONE

As I outlined in previous chapters, for the next five years I went crazy with my newfound wealth. I bought an airplane, a second yacht, traveled extensively, and made a bad loan that caused me to foreclose on a 210-foot ship. My marriage continued to crumble. My restless side needed more, and my relationship with my wife had become like a coma. Stagnation happens to many marriages—but not now, not to me, not in my third go-around. The toys needed upkeep and attention. The travel was very expensive. My cash inflow began to slow, or the outflow increased, or a combination of both happened, so back to work I went.

Going back to work was difficult after the whirlwind lifestyle to which I had grown accustomed. I invested in a hotel, restaurant, and marina project that was doomed from the start and for which I had to spend hours on end, fighting to keep alive. This resulted in heavy borrowing, and I found myself back in debt, making additional cash outlays to service the debt. Just like that, I had gone full circle.

As for my marriage, our time was spent doing things other than what had made the marriage work for so long. Things happened that never should have, and like any difficult situation, both sides had their amount of blame to bear. Nevertheless, after twelve years, the marriage failed; and she got the bank account, the condo, and none of the debt. I got the boat, the ship, the marina, the law practice, and all the debt. My assets were depreciating and required cash outflow, and the debt needed servicing. I found myself virtually broke again. To make matters worse, she asked me to leave the house on my fiftieth birthday. Once again, I found myself on the rocks, and my hull could not take much more—my drowning was near. My law practice was still solid, but to make money there, I had to be at a desk all day; and I could not enjoy life like I thought I needed to do. I was a complete failure, and there was no way to argue to the contrary.

My weaknesses, the abandonment of my grandfather's teachings, and my resultant bad choices were all my fault. I had no one to blame but myself. I had been raised better and had been given the tools to be a success, but I blew it. I had fallen victim to the glimmer and gleam of the fast life—the so-called good life—and in doing so, I learned that it takes a better man than I to have that success and to be able to live within the teachings that I had received. I could not change any of that, so I had to learn to live with my failures. I must have been an expert at that by now; but just when you think you are at the bottom, the earth opens, and you fall deeper. This was about to happen to me.

The twelve years of suspended animation were finally over, and things were once again in turmoil. However, I had almost gotten it right this time around. I had started out with the right attitude and had gone in the right direction. However, the self-indulgence and ego again raised their ugly heads. My successes had been "all mine"; and I had disregarded the help, input, and influence of those around me. Their support, aid, and work had not been part of my thought process. Therefore, my achievements had been "self-achievements," and the roller-coaster ride had begun again.

Clearly, I had been the mover and shaker and had created the overall plan for each project. However, everything in life is a team event. This may not be true in execution, but it is in planning and preparation or even just with one's approach to emotional/mental support and faith. Ignoring this attitude, I was once again mentally alone and only thought about things as they affected my goals and me. This self-centered mind-set was the beginning of my next tragedy. Some people never learn—and I was one of these people.

CHAPTER 7

SNAP, CRACKLE, AND POP

Coincidental to my divorce, I was involved with closing a very large real estate deal. The sellers in the real estate deal decided that they did not get enough money for the land and sued everyone remotely associated with the transaction, including my firm and me for $25,000,000.00. My last bastion of hope—my reputation as an attorney—had disappeared in a split second. Regardless of the explanation, the small-town minds of the time wanted and got a soap opera. As we all know, soap operas are better if you at least dream that the scenes are true. Regardless of the facts of the transaction, the vultures took over, and even my law partners abandoned me. I was all alone and truly without anything except for the tenuous relationship with my girlfriend. At least I still had her, and with that, maybe I could start again.

This suit and the damage caused by an article sent to the paper by the opposing attorney, which was very harsh and unfounded, was that last stick of wood too many that had been thrown on my cart. My cart broke, and what pieces of my entire life that were left crumbled to the ground.

I liquidated what little I had left, packed my bags, and moved to my boat. Lonely was not how I would describe how I felt. I felt as if everyone that I had known knew that I had died, and before I could meet anyone else, I had been locked up in a ten-by-ten-by-seven-foot cell with no light. I had no one to call, no one to lean on, and no hope of anyone finding me because no one knew I existed. That was my life. I did, however, have one friend; and she was my love. Unfortunately, I easily saw that the pressure of my small town was shutting her down slowly but surely. She knew she would have to deal with the locals on a regular basis, would be asked about me daily, probably would have to give a deposition, and generally would be embarrassed to know me. I was truly afraid that I had already lost her, and in fact, that was the case. As each day passed, she became less and less interested in us, and it got to the point where she would not even stop whatever she had been doing when I called. She talked to me as if I was a telemarketer that she did not want to be rude to. It was the pits. I had to get lost in something—my boat, a project, a new career, something. I had to find a way to get it together.

CHAPTER 8

REALIZATION

As I fell deeper and deeper into a bottomless pit, I tried to count what blessings I had left. My sister loved me, I still had a tentative relationship with my love, I had my health most of the time, and I had my mind and the foundation in the three principles with which I had been raised. That was all I had. As to my health, the stress of the recent events had elevated my blood pressure to a dangerous level. For fifty years, my blood pressure had been 110 over 70, and now it was 149 over 95. Even my health was leaving me. I had gained weight, was out of shape, and was drinking too much. Had I ever been a drug user, I am sure that I would have returned to that habit; thankfully, that was one of the few habits that I had never picked up.

I also had little materially. I had my car, my heavily mortgaged yacht, and a few thousand dollars. I had my United States Coast Guard masters license for fifty-ton vessels and could at least turn to that for money if I needed to. I loved the sea and the islands and had always dreamed of cutting the lines and sailing to paradise, but the conservative side of my brain never let me. I had cruised many trips but always on a schedule and never in the leisurely manner that one needs to really enjoy it and do it safely. Maybe that was it. Maybe I needed to change venues and start again in the tropics. Could that be possible?

Clearly, it was possible. I had a very seaworthy vessel; and I had the skills, the experience, and just enough money to make it work. I questioned my sanity for a couple of days and then realized that almost all of my decisions in the past had been bad decisions. Either I was due for a change, or I would make one more bad decision. As I saw it, I had nothing to lose. The only questions were where and with whom. The Bahamas was not original enough and was too much like the environment I was leaving. The Mexican coast was tempting, but the language barrier and the authorities would cause too many problems for me to deal with in my state of mind. That left isolated islands like Jamaica, Grand Cayman, the Dominican Republic, or the Leewards and the Windwards. The latter seemed the best place to go. The atmosphere is great, there are many islands to hop back and forth on, and the locals generally deal well with people with my accent and lack of foreign language skills. So now, who would go? Could I do this alone? Should I do this alone? The second question was easy to answer: *no*. I had to find someone to go with me. With no friends or family, this became a stumbling block. I trusted that as I readied the vessel, my crew would find me. So forward I went.

CHAPTER 9

THE TRIP PLAN: RUNNING AWAY!

To prepare a vessel for such a long and difficult trip required tedious planning and preparation. Detail after detail had to be tended to, or the trip would be a disaster. The engines were first and included cleaning the oil coolers and aftercoolers; replacing all hoses, filters, impellers, and belts; and conducting a general engine review. The fuel had to be cleaned, and my Racor system cleaned and rebuilt. Next came the pumps thru hulls, props, shafts, and steering, which all had to be removed, repaired, and reinstalled. This has to be done in a shipyard while the boat was out of the water. While being serviced there, I had the bottom painted, the hull waxed, and the props removed and retooled to grade-1 status.

Next were the electronics. I bought a new system and tested it thoroughly. I purchased charts and had data chips installed into the navigational equipment. Then the course had to be laid out based on the destination, fuel-consumption rate, sites, and locations that would be handy as ports for repairs and reprovisioning as well as for pure and simple enjoyment of the natural beauty.

I accomplished all of this in record time and within my budget and, while doing so, totally forgot about my problems. As my true love has said many times, this project got me off my "pity porch." Now that the work was done, my nerves began to feel both the excitement and fear that naturally comes with such a long trip and a drastic change of life. I reviewed my trip plan, read all of the cruising guides, and decided on my departure timetable based on the information in the guides. I worked every day on finding my crew and had given up on securing free personnel. I realized that I was such a loser that I had to find the money to pay the crew to go on the trip of a lifetime. Most people would have had fifty people begging to go, but instead, I had to go to a crewing agency to buy friends for the trip.

Out of five candidates, I chose a seventy-year-old tugboat deckhand who had a captain's license and fifty years of experience on the sea. I felt like I could get along with him. He had chartered in the Virgin Islands in the '70s and wanted to go back. The situation seemed perfect, but his fees cut into my budget. We still needed a third deckhand, cook, and general "fetch it" guy. Normally, these guys are a dime a dozen; but it was the end of the yachting season in the Caribbean, and crew were heading to the Mediterranean or back to the States. No one was heading south, and with hurricane season approaching, finding someone was not easy. Two days before the departure date, a friend of mine met a young man who lived on his sailboat and wanted an adventure to the Caribbean. He agreed to go for very nominal wages plus expenses. I hired him sight unseen, and we were set.

During the two weeks before our departure, the winds were a steady northeast, twenty to twenty-five knots; and the waves were enormous. Normally, the weather will clock around in a few days and take the wind to the east, southeast, and then south as the fronts come and go. As the wind changes direction, the seas lie down, and passages such as mine begin. Not this time. The wind remained steady and showed no sign of clocking, which was the situation the morning of our departure date. We checked the weather, both on the machines and by stepping outside and looking. It was bad; it had been bad and was predicted to remain bad. I was paying the crew to sit there plus expenses. I needed to get something moving and to take my mind off all of the problems in my life. We had a crew meeting and voted unanimously to go. The lines were thrown, the route set up in the computers, the interior tied down; and off we went on the windy, rainy morning of March 30, 2007.

CHAPTER 10

PLAN EXECUTION:
THE MOMENT OF TRUTH OR DARE

As I woke up on that fateful morning, I began to question the trip itself, my preparations, and whether the crew would get along. Did I have enough spare parts, and did I have the right ones? Would the pumps hold out if we were holed? Should I have spent the money and the core charge to bring along a spare starter like I had planned to but could not afford to? Would the fifteen-year-old air conditioners make it? They were old and had seen better days. These questions haunted me as I listened to the waves lap against the hull that was being pushed hard by the heavy winds. This was nothing like the beating she would get out there, but in the quiet early morning, it was enough to make me think about all aspects of the trip.

As our nose stuck out into the normally beautiful waters of Hawk's Channel, I knew it was going to be a bad day. Our first leg was 110 nautical miles, or about 128 statute miles, on a northeast course across the Gulf Stream. That, along with a twenty- to twenty-five-knot northeast wind that had blown constantly for ten to twelve days, added up to another bad choice on my part. When up, the Gulf Stream is a world in its own right. Combine that with the natural waves and wind that would be on any body of water under these conditions, and we had a recipe for a very rough ride.

My yacht is sixty-two feet overall, with a fifty-five-foot waterline. She has a deep V hull design with large spray rails. The forward windows had been replaced with fiberglass to avoid any damage from heavy seas. All equipment was duplicated for safety. Its previous owner had run it from Fort Lauderdale to Venezuela to Belize and back every year and obviously had done just fine. The vessel did not worry me. My skills did not worry me, and the man I hired to help me had fifty years of experience. Nevertheless, since nothing had gone right for a long time, I had no reason to expect that trend to change. As we moved northeast, I began to think ahead to all of the problems that could arise so that I would be prepared to deal with them as they arose as I unfortunately believed they were coming.

Nevertheless, the trip coined the Southern Adventure had begun and in grand style—what other way was there to go?

CHAPTER 11

THE TRIP

We navigated east, then east-northeast, then northeast up the channel. The channel is protected by a long reef with some of the most beautiful coral in the United States. Thank God the reef was there because the seas beyond were very unforgiving. However, the farther north we got, the closer we got to the point where we had to leave the protection of the reef and head to sea. I was very uneasy about this, and I could feel the same in the crew. We all knew what we were heading for, but no one spoke about it. Finally, we were there. We had to leave the womb, and out we went.

This entire area has been the topic of many TV shows and documentaries concerning missing boats, planes, and ships. The Bermuda Triangle or Devil's Triangle was, in my mind, a myth and nothing more than a rough area to navigate—one that caused normal human error resulting in loss. Many believe differently, and such thoughts entered my mind way too frequently as we took our first six-foot wave.

The seas were a full six to eight feet on a two- to three-second interval. The boat would rise and fall, lie over, and do it all over again. The total cycle was about ten to twelve seconds. The balance of the trip to the first port was about seven more hours, and if you do the math, you would realize why we were not happy campers. The sea did not let up. We anticipated that as we got closer to the Bahama bank, we would move out of the Gulf Stream and get some lee from small islands such as Bimini for some relief. But this was not to be. The seas stayed with us until we reached the twenty-five-foot waters off the bank at the cut between Gun Cay and Cat Cay.

Many seamen reading this will laugh and comment that they have been in what I have described many times and have stories of the sea far worse than what we encountered. I agree and understand; however, in a noncommercial vessel where pleasure and relaxation was the name of the game, we were in a nightmare. We could have and would have survived a worse situation, even in my boat, but we sure would have rather not.

As we rounded the southern tip of Gun Cay, the red lighthouse was proof that we were about to port and experience the safety it provided. We finally relaxed. We called in, got a slip, and settled in for the night and a good meal. However, as we rinsed off the vessel, we saw what the seas had done. First, the rub rails had been completely torn off from the pressure of the waves rushing up the face of the bow. The forward hatch nearly flooded the forward stateroom, the windlass had virtually stayed underwater the entire time, and the salt water had damaged it to the point that it would not run; the davit motor was soaked even though the motor had been covered and tied off, and the contents of the vessel were as if a milk shake had been made from them. We had secured everything but items in drawers, the refrigerator, the freezer, cabinets, and other compartments that could not be secured, which were a mess. Clothes came off hangers. The tool cabinet had given way to the weight of the tools and had opened—spilling tools, screws, nuts, bolts, and everything imaginable into the floor. It was a mess. Clearly, the next day would be a day of repairs; but now, to the showers and dinner.

Dinner at Cat Cay is always wonderful, and this night was no exception. After dinner, it was not long until bed to end a very hard day. The next morning, we all pitched in and got the vessel in tip-top shape, spending most of the time on the inside and the rub rail. The windlass could not be prepared. It had gotten so covered with salt that it needed to be removed and rebuilt, which was a Nassau project, and we left it till then. We cooked the next night and readied ourselves for the next leg.

On May 2, we headed for Nassau. This leg took us across the bank, an area of beautiful green water over a white-sand floor. The floor is covered with starfish and coral, and the water is so clear that one can photograph the seafloor and get a picture that you'd get if you had been scuba diving. Because of the shallow water, the seas usually stay relatively flat and are not a problem unless the weather totally deteriorates. After the bank, you enter the Tongue of the Ocean. This is a very deepwater area that extends from near Chub Cay south to the southern area of the Bahamas. It is in this body of water that Nassau exists. Because of the depth, large cruise ships can bombard the capital of the Bahamas and double its population from 6:00 a.m. until 6:00 p.m. most days of the season. Although this body of water can and does get rough, this portion of the trip is only forty-five miles.

On our day to cross this expanse, the winds were still high; the normally calm waters of the bank were three to five, and we were taking spray all the way up in the flybridge. Although not dangerous, it was very uncomfortable. The trip would take twelve hours, a very long twelve hours because we hit a large storm and were rained on for the entire trip, forcing us to run exclusively on radar. That was stressful. The seas in the Tongue of the Ocean reminded us of our last leg and were no less punishing. We arrived into Nassau at 6:00 p.m., tied up, ate, and then to bed. The next day, we found the rub rail again torn off; this time, the longer and larger screws had been pushed back and forth against the hull, causing a very large area of nonstructural but visible damage to the vessel. It looked horrible. We repaired that, removed the windlass, and took it to be rebuilt, cleaned her up again, and got ready to go. The windlass was mounted with the motor horizontal under the deck in the chain locker. Getting it in and out was quite a task unless you are three feet tall with six-foot arms and the agility of a ballerina. Obviously, none of us fit that description, so it was a very difficult job. In the end, the windlass was working again and ready for action.

Our next leg would take us deep into the Exumas. I had a friend who knew of a private island being developed as a private resort. It was unfinished but had an operable marina and was located the perfect distance for us on this day of travel. I got permission to dock there for the night and headed for this retreat. After a day of travel on the bank with only two- to four-foot waves—a great day for us, but a relatively rough day for this area—we arrived. The place, owned solely by one man, was paradise. He had a fuel facility, cabins near completion, a first-class marina, an airstrip, and all the amenities that one would expect upon completion. We were greeted by the father-in-law of the owner and were given the tour. It was wonderful. We cooked dinner and rested. The seas appeared to be lying down, and the next day on the water would be an improvement.

Our next leg would be difficult. We would depart and exit to the east of the Exumas off to Clarence Town, Long Island. Here, we would refuel, rest, eat, and depart for a twenty-four-hour run to the Turks and Caicos. All in all, it would be a thirty-six-hour adventure and, if the past few days were an indicator, would be full of excitement.

We departed at 7:00 a.m. the next day. The seas were no more than one to three, and all was great. We made Clarence Town by 4:00 p.m., refueled, filled our water tanks, ate, checked our e-mails, and headed out again. We left at 6:00 p.m. and had a wonderful sunset and smooth sailing. We did shifts, and I pulled the first one. Each shift was three hours, and I got us to the top of the Acklins, and then the captain took over. He was to take us along the north coast of the Acklins then cut south between the Acklins and Plana Cays, below Mayaguana to the Turks and Caicos. As I left my shift, all was well, and I went to bed. After only one hour, water was all over my stateroom, and the seas were frightful—no less than six to eight and confused. The boat would rise up on a wave, and only God knew whether we would fall to port or starboard as the wave passed under the vessel. This went on for the balance of the trip. I came back on shift at 4:00 a.m. after virtually no sleep. We arrived at the bank at about 9:00 a.m., perfect timing to make the passage. The sun would be high enough to show the many coral heads just waiting to gouge the hull or foul the props. The captain had made this passage many years ago in a commercial vessel. He insisted we run south of the charted route into an unsurveyed area. I objected at first but then decided that experience was more valuable than pride and let him have his way. His route, although uncharted, proved to be flawless. We saw no coral heads and made it to port very easily. We docked and headed for the bar. I got in very late that night and felt very poor the next morning.

Nevertheless, we had repairs to do and began promptly. I found the leak into the aft stateroom and repaired it, stopped the forward cabin leak, and got everything in good order. We planned to leave the next morning and cleared out with customs. At 7:00 a.m., we fired the engines, but the starboard engine would not start. We tried everything to no avail. Per our luck, it was a holiday on the island, and the Caterpillar dealer next to the boat was closed. Later that day, the engineer of the local police boat stopped by as he had heard that we were having trouble. He came aboard and found the problem immediately. The salt water that had gotten into the boat via the exhaust leak had found its way into the starter and had ruined it. Only a total rebuild or a new starter would get us going again. I called the United States and had one sent, but it would take two to three days to arrive.

By this time, I really needed to see my love. As I mentioned earlier, she was cooling off toward me, and I could not stand the thought of losing her on top of everything else; so I made up an excuse to go home. Once I knew the new starter was on its way, I left them to install it and sent the two off to the Dominican Republic while I went home to see her. We had a wonderful time, and I felt that all was finally back to normal. I flew into Puerto Plata, Dominican Republic, caught up with my boat, and found her in perfect shape.

We stayed in Puerto Plata for a few days and saw both her wonder and her poverty. It was a strange but beautiful combination. After departing Puerto Plata, we headed to Samana. This little town is on the east coast of the Dominican Republic in a deep inlet, which provides great protection from the weather, but was a very poor area. Although the people spoke little to no English, they were very kind and generous. I liked this place and felt very much at home here. The weather continued to pound us and was now in the form of torrential rain. We endured, and we departed for Puerto Rico at 7:00 a.m. the next morning.

To get to Puerto Rico, we had to cross the Mona Passage, known for confused and rough seas. That did not scare us at all because, so far, that was all we had experienced; and Mona Passage would be par for the course. However, something strange happened as we left the inlet—the seas became totally flat, there were no waves and no swells, and the water was completely glassy. About two hours out, I made my normal engine room check and found salt water spraying everywhere. The hose to the aftercooler had blown and was flooding the engine room—and we did not know for how long. With hot engines and while at sea, I made the repair; and after about one hour, we were under way again. However, this delay would prevent us from making Ponce before dark. We decided to anchor on the west coast of Puerto Rico and go into port the next morning. We arrived and anchored at about 9 p.m., went immediately to sleep, and woke early the next morning to arrive into Ponce before noon. Here, we refueled and relaxed for the rest of that day and the next.

We left early the next morning for St. Thomas in the U.S. Virgin Islands. It was an easy run, and we arrived before 4:00 p.m. We got all our paperwork done, cleaned the boat, and prepared a wonderful meal from the king mackerel that we had caught along the way. We went to bed and visited the island the next day. The next morning, before leaving for town, we were about to start the engines to make sure the new starter was working—and it was—but the port engine would not start. The water that had sprayed out over the Mona Passage had finally ruined the port starter. We found a company that could rebuild this unit since getting another starter would take a week, and late the next day, it was ready. So an unexpected stay in St. Thomas continued our streak of bad luck.

We finally left and headed for the British Virgin Islands. I had been to all of our previous stops by my boat, cruise ship, or plane. Although coming with my own vessel improved the visits, I had never been in awe of anywhere that I had seen. The BVI was my first stop to a place that I had never been to, and I was excited. The rain and heavy clouds notwithstanding, we went into West End to clear where we had our first difficult customs experience. They boarded us and searched every drawer, cabinet, and piece of luggage. Of course, they found nothing, but it took two hours and was very stressful. They finally cleared us, and we left for Road Town, Tortola. We arrived there by 2:00 p.m., docked, had lunch, and then hired a taxi to show us the island. It was a great trip, but after the sightseeing, I was ready to leave.

The next morning, we headed for the Bitter End Yacht Club. I had heard about it but could never have imagined its beauty. My camera was hot to the touch from all the pictures that I took as we pulled into port. As we entered the Bitter End Yacht Club, my amazement grew. Every building seemed to blend perfectly into the natural beauty of the landscape. It was fabulous. The water shimmered like light green emeralds as the wind rippled the surface of the water in the bay.

We tied up and watched one of the many bare boaters attempt to dock a boat way too large and complicated for a novice weekend vacationer to handle. We laughed to ourselves that the stories told back home will make him look like Blackbeard when in reality, he looked like a Captain Ron without experience.

We checked in, checked the weather, and started our exploration of the club and its amenities. As we had earlier navigated northeast from Road Town thru the Sir Francis Drake Channel, we passed

Peter Island, home of a very exclusive resort, and Fallen Jerusalem, a rock formation/island chain that looks like the ruins of a great ancient city. We also passed the Baths, a rock formation consisting of weathered, seaworn boulders larger that the average home. The rocks sit on one another as if a monster dump truck had unloaded a pile of very large gravel. The captain explained that from the shore, one could wind oneself thru the crevices of the boulders and find many shallow pools of seawater on which refracted rays of light created some of the most scenic sights one could imagine. As I explored Bitter End, I kept wondering of the explanation for this wonder and sought out the concierge to arrange a trip to see it.

The Bitter End Yacht Club is on the northeasternmost tip of Virgin Gorda. To my knowledge, it is accessible only by boat. To get to the Baths on the very southeast side of the island, we had to arrange for a water taxi. The club provided the service free of cost to a settlement on the west side of the bay where a land taxi could be hailed.

The taxi driver took us along the center of the very narrow and picturesque island, allowing us to photograph the emerald green waters of the Drake Channel on the north and the indigo waters of the Caribbean Sea on the south. Although a picture speaks a thousand words, we needed a five-gigabyte chip to describe the beauty of the scenery. We arrived at the Baths and found that we had quite a long hike down to the entrance. Once there, we then learned that the journey thru the boulders and the small crevices, voids, and ponds would take twenty minutes and a lot of energy and dexterity. The captain, who wanted to revisit this landmark again after twenty-five years, felt he was not physically able to make the trip and stayed behind. This saddened me, and I realized once again that one has to grab the gusto whenever possible as there is no catching up once life passes you by.

The mate and myself journeyed on and finally found the area where the boulders met the sea. The site was all it was made out to be, and the photos we took are some of my favorite of the entire trip. Describing the scenery would be too difficult, so I will not try. Look it up on the Net and see for yourselves. Several vessels had anchored off the coast, and the crew had swum in to view the site. I was not interested in this approach as the swells that day were very large, and the thought of leaving the boat at anchor with Mother

Nature pushing as hard as she could to put the vessel on those large rocks was very unpleasant. My experiences have taught me that Mother Nature wins more than she loses, and I was relieved that we had taken a taxi.

We departed for the boat after about a two-hour stay, ate a wonderful meal at the club, and planned our last leg. The last leg was the Anegada Passage (a.k.a. Sombrero Passage to some). The locals refer to this area as the Oh My God Passage. The natural swell direction is southwest, and the seas funnel into a ninety-mile-wide opening between Sombrero Cay and the BVI, causing very large swells and confused waters. To go anywhere in the leewards, one must travel southeast, which puts the seas on your beam or quarter at best. The swells are a usual five to seven and much higher on a bad day. Furthermore, the swells are constant, and there is no lee to take shelter.

You know the rest of the story by now. The winds were still blowing out of the east at twenty to twenty-five, and five to seven footers were nothing more than a dream to us. Since the forecast period available showed no change, we decided to go ahead and finish the trip. One more bad day at sea beats a good day at work, and we left at 6:00 a.m. the next morning.

We untied and were under way. We left the bay to the northwest, turned north, went around the tip of Virgin Gorda, and then turned southeast toward Anguilla. This would be the start of the ninety-mile marathon. We were just about to round the top of the island when I made a routine engine room check and found the raw water pump leaking badly. We cut the engine, and given the sea state and engine heat, an at-sea repair was out of the question. So back to the bay we went. Once at anchor, I discovered that the problem was caused by bad zinc, and the repair was quick and easy. We went back at it and had lost only one and a half hours.

As we rounded the tip of Virgin Gorda and turned southeast, reality was in the form of eight to twelve footers with a very short interval. These would be fun if you were a stuntman or bull rider. But since none of us fit these categories, we buckled down for a beating. The refrigerator slid out of its cradle, the ice maker flipped upside down, the mattresses came off the beds, and then everything else that has been described in other rough passages repeated themselves. We had to back her down to 1,750 rpm rather than the

2,400 I normally ran my Cat 3208s at, and our speed then fell to eight to nine knots rather than the twelve to thirteen she normally cruised at. This added time to the marathon bull ride, but it helped keep the vessel in one piece. We finally caught some lee just south of Anguilla, slipped into Simpson Bay, St. Maarten, and dropped anchor about 5:00 p.m. The boat was a wreck, and we were dead tired. We rested, showered, ate, and slept.

The next morning, we cleared customs and began cleaning up the vessel.

I had finally arrived, the culmination of a lot of planning, work, and dreaming. I had done it and in grand style. With everything else in my life, it had not been easy but was well worth it. Now what to do? I was in a strange country with no friends and no job. That was the daunting part of all of it. I had always fancied myself as James Bond, but now I felt like Maxwell Smart (for those of you who remember that TV show). I had some thinking to do.

I arranged a trip home to see my girlfriend and to bring her down to see my new world. The trip went well, and while in the islands, we discussed our future in a very serious and positive manner. It looked like she and I were going to make it, and that was my foundation that I needed to build my goal and my dream. Once she left, I began to plan a future for myself and with her. I was stable again.

Over the next few weeks, the lawsuit continued to drag on, and I had to return home for a deposition. Going home would have been fine, but I had been hired in the meantime to bring down another vessel from Fort Lauderdale to St. Maarten. I was to leave on June 10. The vessel was an eight-knot Grand Banks, and the trip would be over the same course, with different stops because of the speed. Many of the legs would have to be twenty-four-hour ones to get to a safe port during daylight hours. This took some planning and would be a much harder trip on the crew. If the weather cooperated, somehow, the two would cancel each other out.

My attorneys got the deposition delayed, and off I went on another adventure. This time, I was being paid and had no expenses, and my stuff was not rolling around the floors of the cabins.

I flew into Lauderdale and met up with my girlfriend. We had a great weekend, and she was to meet me midtrip in St. Thomas. Everything seemed to be getting better and better. I was sad on the day she left, and the trip ahead was daunting. The more I thought of the many twenty-four- and thirty-six-hour legs, the more I realized that the trip would be hard work. The whole gang met together on Sunday night; and the planning, provisioning, repairing, plotting, and organizing began. On Friday, we sea-trialed the vessel, fueled her up, and were ready for a 6:00 a.m. departure.

As I left port, I did not know that I would probably never see my love again and that over the next three weeks, my life would take a 180-degree turn. What a trip this was going to be.

My girlfriend and I talked on the phone daily, but the calls grew cooler, and the conversations became more scripted and forced than warm and loving. Something was brewing, and I was unable to carry on a decent conversation because of the limitations of satellite phones and e-mail at sea. By the time we got to Clarence Town, Long Island, in the Bahamas, she dropped the news to me that we were over. She gave me all sorts of reasons, but none made sense, which made things even worse.

Our trip to Clarence Town had been routine. We ran the first leg of Fort Lauderdale to Nassau in one twenty-four-hour stretch, had normal weather, and encountered no problems. We laid over in Nassau for the balance of our day of arrival and the next day to see the sights of Atlantis and the Nassau area. As usual, the aquarium in the Atlantis was breathtaking; and this time, we went to the predator tank and tunnel, which were awesome. We left for our next venue early the next morning.

Norman's Cay in the upper Exumas in the '60s and early '70s was an exclusive resort with a private landing strip, club, and rental cabins. The drug dealer Carlos Lehder of the Medellín Cartel arrived in the late '70s, took over the island, and used it as a staging ground for drug entry into the United States. The Bahamian government did little to stop him, and the island became famous for reasons unrelated to it natural beauty. This island was a very scary place during his reign of terror. In July of 1980, a yacht belonging to a retired Fort Myers, Florida, couple was found drifting near the island with a corpse aboard. Lehder harassed the few island inhabitants until all fled, leaving the island completely to him and his illegal project. Since the Bahamian government did nothing to ward off Lehder's takeover of this beautiful island, speculation brewed that huge payoffs were being made, but nothing had ever been proven. Lehder continued his occupation of Norman's Cay until 1982. When the owners reclaimed the island, much had been destroyed, and little remained of the once-plush resort or its pristine reputation.

I have visited the island many times, snorkeled its beautiful waters, and eaten at McDuff's, a very small restaurant and bar located near the western shore and right on the runway. Because of the airstrip, you might see Michael Jordan or Jimmy Buffett eating there on any given day. Upon our arrival, we found that McDuff's was no more. The restaurant was now Norman's Cay Beach Club, and the nephew of the original owners of the island ran it. Norman's Cay Beach Club had been completely refurbished and was gorgeous. We had a great meal after we had snorkeled at a private island, a wrecked airplane, and the beach where we had anchored. All in all, it was a wonderful day on the white sand beaches of Norman's Cay.

Early the next morning, we left for Staniel Cay. We arrived at noon, fueled up, completed the chore of dropping anchor, and launched the dinghy. Once in the dinghy, I took the crew to Thunderball Cave, which from the outside looks like a large rock island. On the west side is an opening that remains underwater except at low tide. If you dive down about three to four feet and swim hard for four to five seconds, you surface into the most beautiful cavern you have ever seen. The main room is about the size of a suite in a five-star hotel. Another cavern is located to the south and is about half this size. The top of the cavern is about thirty feet and has three openings that allow the sun's rays to enter. The water is cool, and the fish swim around as if in a giant fishbowl. This location was used when shooting the movie *Thunderball*. Near the end of the movie, James Bond is locked in an underwater secret bomb storage area and left to die. He sees light and swims to the surface to find that he is in this very cavern. He shoots his flare; the coast guard helicopter sees it, and they drop him a line, saving him. To be in this cave and knowing its history made the experience all that more exhilarating.

We finished our photography session and went back to the boat to rest and get ready for dinner. Dinner was to be at the Staniel Cay Yacht Club, which was a one-seating Bahamian-style dinner. The building is typical for the area with its rustic fisherman's style ambiance. Memorabilia cover the walls, including many photographs of the film crew who shot *Thunderball*. As usual, dinner was wonderful and truly Bahamian. After dinner, we took the dinghy back to the boat and slept.

Our rest period was short because to reach Clarence Town before they closed meant that we had to depart Staniel at 1:30 a.m. We did so and navigated back to the marina, north thru the channel, and out into the ocean. We set our waypoint to the northernmost tip of Long Island and headed southeast.

From Clarence Town, we continued southeast to the Turks and Caicos. This leg was also twenty-four hours and had the potential, as I had experienced, of being brutal. This morning, the trip was tolerable; and we reached the bank at 4:30 a.m., too early to cross, so we anchored for a four-hour nap. Once the sun was high, we crossed the bank using the captain's route that we had used on my prior trip and arrived safely to port by noon.

Having been on the boat incommunicado for twenty-four hours and knowing that I desperately needed to see and talk to my now ex-girlfriend, I hopped on the first plane home. The owner of the boat had agreed that we all needed a rest, and since we were going to lay over for a couple of days anyway, my absence did not interrupt the trip. Upon arriving home, she refused to see me. I packed my personal things from her home and stored them. I begged her to talk to me, and she refused. I left town with a totally broken heart, and I had the roughest legs of the trip ahead of me.

I had to pass thru Fort Lauderdale to get to the boat, and given the flight schedule, I spent one night there. While lying in bed that night, I began to gasp for breath. I was suffocating. I tried everything, but to no avail. My travels from Clarence Town to this point took four days, and I had slept six hours' total during this time. My body had given out; and my mind was working overtime reviewing my hopeless future, my lost love, and my past fifty-one years of failures. My stress and fatigue had brought on a most severe anxiety attack. It was now only midnight, and I somehow had to survive until daylight. I paced, walked outside, and wrote e-mails I knew no one would read or care about. I tried to read, watch TV, exercise, and take a shower—all to no avail. Nevertheless, all of these things passed the time, and morning finally arrived. I called my sister, and she helped me understand that no one's mind was capable of assimilating all of the different issues and problems that I faced, especially with virtually no sleep. She reminded me that in times like these, you simply have to ask God to take over and handle the things we are unable to handle. She told me to create a box in my mind and stuff anything that was overwhelming into that box. Then she told me to lock it and let God handle them while I got some rest, relaxed, and took care of the smaller tasks. I did just that and, in addition, went to the doctor.

The doctor told me the same thing in scientific terms. He could not do anything for me since the only prescription that would have helped me was one for sleeping pills or antidepressants, and without a more thorough exam, he could not prescribe those. I was left to fight alone. I rested most of that day and took some over-the-counter sleeping pills to fall asleep. By the time I got on the plane, I was relaxed and thinking much more clearly. I realized that I had to take one step at a time. I had to first attack the lawsuit and get that behind me. I then had to heal myself. Then, and only then, would I have a fighting chance to deal with my ex-girlfriend. My friends told me that no woman liked a weak, begging, and broken man. I had never been one but knew I had to rid myself of that label before she and I could talk. I got back on the boat and headed to the Dominican Republic.

Our trip took us out across the bank to the ocean just below Grand Turk. We crossed that channel and planned to anchor at Big Sand Cay, a deserted island boasting a host of birds and fish. It is desolate but full of beauty and wonder. We planned to rest, eat, and swim, and then head south to Puerto Plata. At 9:00 p.m., we cranked the engines and roared south.

After clearing the southern tip of the island, it hit us—a ten-foot full beam wave. For those that are unfamiliar with this term, this is when a wave ten feet high hits the vessel directly on her side, causing the vessel to roll. Boats are designed to take such punishment directly head-on, but not on their beam. The weather forecast claimed ten- to fifteen-knot winds with the sea three to five out of the southeast. Little wonder that we were amazed at our fate. Our positive outlook allowed us to assume that these seas were the result of the wind whipping around the tip of the island and that the situation would improve the farther south we went. It did not and in fact worsened. I suggested that we simply turn back, go to anchor, and wait out the unexpected winds. We started to make the turn. But the vessel's slow maneuverability and the large beam area that the waves struck us on caused the vessel to almost broach as we attempted our turn. The owner opted to alter course and keep going. As I charted the new course we were forced to take, our next port of call would be San Juan. Getting there would take another thirty hours, and we were on the twelfth hour now. Nothing was working, everything in the vessel had now found at least one new home, and most items had traveled almost everywhere in the boat. Glass had broken, making bare feet impossible and standing virtually impossible. Sleep was only a pipe dream, and eating and drinking were out of the question. For the first time in thirty-five years of boating, I was scared. I called my then ex-girlfriend to advise her of our plight and for moral support. She never responded, checked on me, or gave any indication that she was concerned over my living or dying. This sent me over the edge. I was forced to wake my sister up and at least tell her what was going on; that way, in case we went down, someone would know where to start looking. I hated doing this because I knew she would be up all night—but I had to.

At 4:00 a.m., I took a sleeping pill and got some rest, but no sleep. By the time I arose, the marina was in sight. The other two crew members had gradually turned the boat back to the correct heading, and although we arrived some three hours late, we arrived. Our nerves were shot, our bodies exhausted, and the boat was a shambles.

However, all of that was behind us and soon forgotten once inside the protection of the harbor. We docked, ate, and crashed. Later that day, we toured the island, met the marina owner, and went to a wonderful show in the cabaret and then to the casino. The next day, we hired a guide and saw in detail the beauty of the area. We ate an early dinner and then went to bed. All of this was still pasted on the background of a passage that could have easily taken our lives. That, added to my personal drama, made me more fully appreciate the true beauty of this island.

Our next leg was another thirty-six hours to Ponce, Puerto Rico, over the Mona Channel. This channel laid down for my previous passage, and we prayed for the same luck this time. Our trip across the top of the Dominican Republic went without problems, and darkness fell as we rounded the corner and turned south. The seas were calm, and I was convinced we had hit it right again. At dawn, we had acquired something, causing a very loud noise in the boat's bilge. We were afraid to make the crossing in such a condition, so we altered route and went into Punta Cana on the easternmost tip of the island. We tied up at 6:00 a.m. To our surprise, the noise came from a collection of crab traps that we had inadvertently run over and that had caught the bow and props. The floats were hitting the hull, accounting for the unexplained noise. We cleared the traps and continued.

As we crossed the channel, the seas were three to five. About halfway, they grew quickly to seven to nine, and the wind was at least twenty-five knots. This continued till 8:00 p.m. when we finally arrived in Ponce. The thirty-six-hour leg had been brutal, and we were dead tired. We had not yet gotten over the fatigue from our run to Puerto Plata, and then this. We headed to bed early and then woke early the next morning to deal with customs and immigration. It was 10:30 a.m. before the formalities were over.

The owner wanted to proceed and get to the southeast corner of the island, rest, and then proceed to St. Thomas the following day. With strong winds, this plan seemed a push, but off we went. I charted a route that was close inshore, hoping to get some lee. However, the seas were out of the southeast, and there was no lee. Soon, we were back into ten footers, had no hope of making the 120-degree turn into the marina, and had no choice but to rethink the route. I found an anchorage on the western tip of Vieques Island, which added two more hours but still enabled us to arrive just before darkness. I did not know if we would have enough protection in that location to anchor. Heading there was a gamble that, if wrong, would have forced us to continue throughout the night through some rough seas. We arrived just at dusk; and to our amazement, not only was it well protected from the east wind and southeast swells, it also had moorings. This promised a safe anchorage and a good night's sleep. We ate, counted our blessings, and arose the next morning for our next leg.

Our next leg was a six-hour run to St. Thomas; and although rough, we arrived on time, tied up, and let out a sigh of relief. Once here, we all knew that we could wait out the weather and, if necessary, go home and return once the weather broke. The pressure was off, and the healing could begin.

Once we docked, I checked my e-mail and had several messages from my ex-girlfriend. She was sending mixed signals, starting with language that led me to believe that there was still hope, yet ending with an unequivocal "It's over." This roller-coaster ride after the hard and frightful long trip was taking its toll, and I was again moving toward a bad fall. My fatigue level was high, and my mental condition low. Again, my sister, for the fifth time in three weeks, got me through.

I flew home as did the other two crew members. They later went over and got the boat on a good-weather weekend and safely arrived in their home of St. Maarten. Given the additional airfare and expense, they did this on their own and did not bring me over for that last leg. I have stayed in contact with them, and they are busy refurbishing the vessel and repairing the damage that Mother Nature and Neptune inflicted upon the boat. I wished them well, but I had business to attend to.

I recounted these two adventures for many reasons. First, this drastic lifestyle change was what I needed to open my eyes and see who I had become. While in my stagnant environment, I never saw beyond the end of my nose. How many times have you driven to work and never noticed the houses and businesses along the way? The trip is so routine that you do not see what you would see if you were driving the route for the first time. This was my life. I had to get into a new environment to find myself. The trips were such a drastic contrast to my prior fifty-one years that many of life's treasures and opportunities became apparent to me, ones that had not previously been in my thought processes. The simple pleasures of life such as watching the sunrise or sunset has such a calming effect on the daily stresses of life. Observing people of all cultures deal in different ways with the ever-changing world was fascinating and refreshing. Learning that we are such an insignificant piece of the large world was daunting. We get so tied up in our little worlds that we become larger and seem more important to ourselves and others than we ever are. These and many other truths, which I had given lip service to over the years, were things that I truly experienced and enjoyed.

Second, I began to see the true wonders and natural beauty in our world. Seeing such beauty led me to better understand that man is not the greatest thing on this earth, nor has he ever created anything as beautiful and as well functioning as what I saw on the trips. I reexamined my faith, which showed me that, clearly, a higher power is in charge of our existence. This altered, for the better, my view of myself, the world, and everything in it. Therefore, I relate my experiences as best as I can in the hope that readers may experience some of the same realizations that I did. The world, and our actions and existence in it, has a much broader and expansive effect than we could ever know. That understanding is critical to effecting any type of change that we drastically need.

I am back in reality now, and my adventures are over. As I relived this life story while preparing to write this book, I found many of the answers to the questions that started this literary project. Why are we so unhappy? What has gone wrong?

CHAPTER 12

FACING REALITY

As my adventures show, hiding or running from your problems only heightens the effect and solves nothing. In fact, running proves that even the adventure of a lifetime can be ruined if you don't deal with your problems head-on. The easy way out is never the right way out.

This conclusion well learned, I secured my yacht and headed back to the States. After about a week, I was back in the States—lost but, at the same time, ready to reestablish myself. I stayed at my sister's house until I was stable. While there, I prepared my resume and began to find my new life course. With my sister's guidance, I started reconnecting the dots between my life and God's influence on me. Simply put, I finally realized that I cannot operate solely based on my own talents, intelligence, and physical ability. Without God's guidance and direction, I am lonely, helpless, and without purpose.

This lesson was engraved in my early childhood, but over the course of a long and hard fifty-one years, I had let my ego and false sense of importance push aside this most important life lesson of all. As I reflected over my life, I questioned each phase and asked myself about the different turns that my life would have taken had I applied this refound life principle at each juncture in my life. In each case, I saw that I could have avoided every failure. Moreover, that my God-given talents could have been focused and used for much more important purposes was evident to me.

I then pondered why such a well-learned principle did not influence me when I most needed it. To investigate this question, I thought of the many times that I have scorned criminals, psychos, and other degenerate people who—only when faced with criminal conviction, death, or a terminal disease—suddenly find religion. I would say to myself, "That's convenient!" That these people could do whatever they wanted, live the life of the devil, and, then in their last hour, "find religion" and hope to avoid the final judgment seemed ironic. I called such people hypocrites and opportunists. Of course, the shoe is now on the other foot. I have come to understand that the hard times are what force us to think in a way that is more pure and real. We realize that we cannot do anything alone and that we are weak and frail when acting alone. I am not a criminal, but I have not lived a life that I am very proud of as it has been virtually godless. Moreover, when faced with my seemingly insurmountable problems, I was finally able to see the real meaning and purpose of God's teachings. Simply put, when all is going well, his lessons are difficult to put into perspective. Moreover, seeing how fortunate we each are is difficult. Realizing how wonderful each of our particular God-given talents are and the preciousness of each talent is not easy. Particularly in our world of prosperity, seeing how really helpless and hopeless each of us are on an individual basis is almost impossible. We do not give credit to or acknowledge the support and aid that those around us, and God, give to each of us. We each take too much credit for our achievements and way too little for our failures. We tend to see everything with a "me" mentality rather than a "team" mentality.

As I reflect on my positive achievements, in each case, I can clearly point to the tremendous help from others and what we call luck than direct actions of my own in ascertaining where credit is due. Without the help of others and those random occurrences of luck, all of my achievements would have been either failures or not nearly the successes they were. Try it. Better yet, spend a Sunday afternoon watching a football game, particularly a game with NFL stars. Watch for any touchdown, tackle, catch, or other spotlight play that would have happened without the aid of the other athletes on the field. Would such a play have happened without the detailed game plans designed by the coaches? What about the training and weight work forced upon the players by the assistant coaches in the off-season? What about the weather or the random events that happen on any given day or the calls by the referees? Do not all of these factors affect each play every Sunday?

Such an exercise is not to say that every athlete on the field is not gifted or is not the cream of the crop, but it takes more than talent to be a success. We should just recognize that it is impossible to say that any of them do it all themselves. We all rely on others every day, and we are nothing without that aid and comfort. Imagine the best quarterback or running back in the league trying to play another NFL team alone. The game would result in a massacre and would not last ten minutes before the star was reduced to a pile of bruised, broken bones. The same applies to us. This is the easiest lesson in life but, when in the midst of success, is one of the hardest to remember.

CHAPTER 13

APPLIED LESSONS

Now that I've played out my first fifty-two years, let's see how the lessons now learned could have altered, lessened, or avoided the miscues in my life.

Generally, I was too motivated. I only thought of hard work and getting good grades. Achievement was my only goal. I never learned to appreciate downtime and life itself. Goals were instilled in me, and I went from goal to goal, not day to day. As I now look back, my grandfather saw this trait and urged moderation upon me. However, I understood his urgings to apply only to partying, drinking, and other fun activities. I never understood that he was telling me that too much of anything, good or bad, is unhealthy.

In our world today, many of us are driven too long and too hard to achieve. From sports to studies, our parents strive for perfection. Our parents attend all of our sports practice sessions, games, and events and accept nothing but winning. We have forgotten that these are just games that kids play for fun and exercise. We want too much and are therefore forced to push too hard to achieve and to have more. Both parents work and still don't have enough. The price of success has gotten too high, and we enjoy nothing. We are raising our children to achieve good grades, participate in extracurricular activities, excel in sports, attend the best schools, take the best classes, and wear the best clothes, drive the best cars, and use the best electronics. To what end is this endless pursuit? Are our children happier than we were as kids? Are they better adjusted? Did we have mass killings in our schools years ago? Does a degree from Harvard or Yale make one a better or happier person? These are real issues. Careful and honest analysis will result in some very interesting answers. Each person must perform this analysis on himself or herself, but the answers are clear.

Executive headhunters and human resources departments in major corporations have created a profile that they believe describes the best prospects. The profile incorporates the criteria and characteristics listed above. As a result, we are driven to fit into this profile, thus begins the vicious circle. I know hundreds of excellent executives and businesspeople who have excelled with their state college degrees or even without any college degree. I played on a fairly level field during my career with a degree from a school that lacked the prestige of the most exclusive schools. I believe that your ultimate success depends on who you really are and the values and character you carry with you, regardless of the school you attended or the awards that were bestowed upon you as a student. The awards, grades, and, ultimately, the volume of knowledge that you truly learn all follow behind your values and your character. One can learn at any school if the desire and commitment are there. Further, your interpersonal skills play a large role in your day-to-day success, which is why I spent so much time early in this book addressing what I perceive as a decay in such skills.

Money is clearly a measure of success, but it is only one of many such measures. People who measure success only by monetary criteria fall short in the big picture of life. Money and material things are so coveted and glamorous, making monetary scales the easiest and most understood standards with which to judge our day-to-day success. However, character, loyalty, care, and concern for others should be the real measuring stick. Teachers, firefighters, hospital workers, volunteers, policemen, and the like, are the people that, day in and day out, make life more livable and better for everyone. They keep the rest of us going and keep us safe. Yet we attach large paychecks to salesmen, attorneys, corporate executives, accountants, and the like, and lower pay scales to these less glamorous but very important jobs. If we were to redesign the measures of success, it would be interesting to see which jobs would change in terms of pay rates. We pay attorneys and accountants large sums of money to find loopholes, to avoid laws and regulations, or to negotiate special deals or obtain special consideration in a particular business deal. From a higher perspective, this kind of pay for manipulation seems blatantly wrong and unfair; however, these are the professions that so many of our children are pushing so hard to attain.

Men and women seek out the most gorgeous specimens of the opposite sex as their mates and seldom consider, until it is too late, that the inner person is the most important aspect of choosing a lifelong partner. Typically, the most handsome or beautiful man or woman has been chased and pampered during his or her entire life because of his or her physical attributes and has gotten breaks in school, job interviews, promotions, and in life in general. Although many exceptions to this stereotype exist, most often, we do not discover the good or bad inner qualities until the physical attraction has brought about a long-term relationship or marriage. Again, we have become such a shallow society that it is no wonder that our divorce rates are at an all-time high, and suicide rates and tragic crimes among children shock us every day.

The majority of the people in today's world are missing the target, which is family, true loving relationships, character, and hard work. These values are important yet are not what people strive for. But should they not be? Isn't it true that when you are happy that everything comes easier and that hard times are easier to accept and deal with? Would success, measured by any scale, not come easier to a person who is happy and well grounded? And if that is true, does that not dictate that our goals need to be redefined? I know that in my life, which is not untypical, had I had proper goals, I would have avoided many tragedies.

We as a society need to step back and reassess our entire outlook—a grassroots person-by-person reevaluation. Each person joining the cause will touch others, and the movement will gain momentum. We have to start somewhere, it has to be started by someone, and it must grow until it is like a huge game of dominos. Our leaders, churches, teachers, and parents have to make this move.

Once we have a higher perspective, we can then focus on our financial situation. We will be able to reschedule our priorities, which in turn will magically solve many of our personal and national financial problems and crises.

I am not asking or suggesting that we lower our goals or accept mediocrity. However, when the standard or scale becomes broader than just monetary and includes other criteria, we can then achieve our financial goals, which would have built-in happiness to make the vicious circle less vicious. With family happiness and inner peace, we would be able to relax and think better and more broadly. Such thinking cannot but help us be even more successful while still enjoying peace and tranquility. We can have our nice things and our indulgences; we simply do not need to worship them and believe that the ownership of such things brings happiness.

If politicians would find a way to set platforms they believe in and fight for if they are elected, our country would once again rise to supremacy. Today, the way to get elected is to find a hot topic, poll who wants what, and then form a campaign platform around that. Politicians do this regardless of what they personally believe. However, this breaks down because it takes a very special person to lead a real fight for a cause he does not believe in. Therefore, when a politician adopts a cause in which he does not believe, the fight will break down when confronting any resistance. In that case, the cause or belief becomes compromised. We are so preoccupied with getting the job that we forget what the job is. It takes a special person to really lead a county, state, or country in a manner that remains in line with his values.

Again, the basic values discussed herein must permeate the political system and override the interests of the lobbyists, the hunger for power and money, and the individual agendas of those holding power. We must begin electing people with character and values. Like everything else, this must be a grassroots campaign and can happen if enough people agree to and understand the importance of this one concept.

The United States of America did not become the greatest country on earth by accident. It happened because of the values and principles so carefully laid out by our founders in the Constitution and the Declaration of Independence. Over the years, we have tried to change these values and principles to make society more like we want it to be rather than what it ought to be. Maybe they had it right hundreds of years ago, and our amendments and current-day desires that conflict therewith need to be reevaluated rather than accepted as ideas better than those of our Founding Fathers.

Taking prayer out of schools, courtrooms, and our day-to-day lives is a serious violation of the initial principles on which this country was founded. A godless society is a crumbling society, and history has proven that time and time again. Why is that lesson so hard to learn yet so easily shown to be accurate from a simple historical review? There are so many other teachings in world history that are forgotten and then relearned. Are we so self-indulgent that we can afford to disregard the value of hundreds of years of teachings? Are we so smart that we can do what history has proven does not work? I do not think so!

In the movie *King Kong*, the islanders from the island on which the massive gorilla lived had built their entire existence around the fear and respect of its destructive power. They built massive forts and fences for protection from the beast. They performed human and animal sacrifices to please the "gods" and to be protected from the rage of the predator. Their everyday lives were constantly affected by his existence. He was then removed from the island and taken to the mainland. Later, the scientists returned to the island and found a shocking situation. The fences and forts were in disrepair. The structure of the society had fallen apart. Most of the islanders were drunks, and sex and sin were rampant. Fiction so often mimics reality. You see, without that common bond and fear, society and the camaraderie of the islanders fell apart. With no fear, the rules had no effect. Without the incentive to follow the rules to avoid the wrath of the beast, people began to step outside the normal boundaries, and chaos began.

Every society must have mutual rules, and people within those societies must exhibit mutual respect to survive. As those basic rules crumble, so does society, whether that society is the local bridge club, golf club, student government, or our country. Once we begin removing these basic principles on which a particular society was created, the effect can be predicted fairly easily.

My point is that character, faith, real values, and a belief of a higher power are critical to our existence and success.

SUMMARY AND CONCLUSION

My life journey is evidence that the influences of the times can completely change the values and directions of one's life. Even when the family unit and home life are strong and appropriate during a child's development, my own life is proof that this foundation may not be enough to deflect the negative trends and motivations that we encounter every day. This fact notwithstanding, without a very supportive and loving childhood, our future generations are terribly at risk.

Our lifestyle and measuring sticks need to reflect true values and admirable goals, which can include monetary elements but must emphasize other important criteria. Our goals should include family, character and ethics, happiness, and monetary success. I believe that money and material things clearly do not equate to happiness. In fact, the pursuit of more money to acquire material things creates a stressful and unhappy environment. Our goal as to material things needs to be to acquire only those things that have function and a clear purpose in our lives so that our acquisition does, in fact, give us pleasure. This is in contrast to simply buying items to keep up with what is popular to be accepted.

Once we find happiness, our perspective and goals will be much easier to set and attain. Once our goals are properly defined and then achieved, our finances should become much more controllable and will not be the driving force that they are in today's society. Again, finances are of the utmost importance; but family and happiness should be the driving forces and the final goals, not the amount of money one has. Remember that although the man who dies with the most toys wins, he is still dead.

Once the general populate can begin to understand the slippery slope that our current way of life leads to, it will be very easy to begin placing the appropriate people in our leadership—people who can address many of the problems of our localities, our states, and our country. But this has to start at home and work outward. Words and deeds have to join hands as words alone will not solve our problems.

This is not a book of religion or is intended to promote such. However, it is my view that we cannot forget or ignore the simple fact that there is a higher power and that such consideration must enter into our daily lives. This country was founded on that principle, and it needs to permeate today's society. As said earlier, just take a history lesson, and this realization will become more apparent to you.

If we each were to set as a personal goal doing something positive and extra each day, however small, to promote a less stressful and more fulfilling environment at work, at home, or at one of our social events, you will be amazed at how quickly the effects will be felt. As an individual, each of our acts is not that significant; but as we work in concert, the masses can accomplish whatever they choose to.

As to myself, I have implemented my philosophy into my life; and although life is never perfect, I am the happiest I have ever been. My outlook and goals remain, but my standards are better designed. I am back on my feet, and I see the big picture. I still have to work every day to keep things in perspective, but anything worth doing is worth doing diligently. By the way, I just got engaged to the wonderful woman whose presence pervaded this book. Life has a way of giving back if we remember the rule that we have to give to get. I learned that lesson and hope to never forget it again.

Finally, I can assure you that since I now know that my hot dogs, hamburgers, and steaks do indeed taste better on a charcoal grill than on gas, I will never engage in the purchase of an expensive, shiny stainless steel status symbol gas grill to impress my neighbors and friends. I do not need it, and only if its function and design were required at some time in the future would I ever consider it. Until then, my inexpensive charcoal grill will do just fine.

Made in the USA
Lexington, KY
16 March 2011